racing on the wind

racing on the wind

by E. and R. S. Radlauer

illustrated with photographs by the authors

Franklin Watts, Inc., 730 Fifth Avenue, New York, N.Y. 10019
Library of Congress Cataloging in Publication Data on page 48
Copyright © 1974 by E. and R. S. Radlauer
Printed in the United States of America

5   4   3   2   1

When the wind blows, many things go. The things and the people in them may go up, down, around, or whatever way the wind goes. They may go over water, on the water, over land, or on land. History is filled with stories of people who used wind and air for fun and travel. One story that goes back about 3,000 years into history tells of two Greek men who escaped from prison by using wings made of feathers and wax. The story says the wax wings melted when one man flew too near the sun. His feathers fell off and he crashed into the sea. If those Greeks had used **hang glide** or **self-soaring** wings for their prison escape, there wouldn't have been any wax for the sun to melt. Of course, no one believes they got near the sun, anyway.

4

This hang-glide flier seems to do fine without feathers and wax for wings.

For self-soaring or hang gliding there should be wind, plenty of it. A wind of 20 miles per hour or more is good for flying. Before flying, a rider sets up his kite at the top of a hill. The kite must be unfolded and set up facing into the wind. If the front or point isn't facing the wind, the kite may go flying without the rider.

Hang glide kites are made of tightly woven cloth, lightweight metal rods, and strong wires. The cloth is so tightly woven that it's almost **airtight**. The rods and wires should be made of very strong material. If something should break during a flight—well remember the Greeks.

People have always wanted to fly, and people have always wanted to add beauty to their lives. Beauty can come from colors, shapes, and forms. Self-soaring people add beauty to their kites with colors and decorations. Quite often a person may have a kite custom-made by a professional kite builder. The kite builder can let the buyer pick the cloth for color and decoration. But when it comes to the shape, the professional builder doesn't let the buyer have much say. A kite has to be built to fly. That's why the shape is important. People who build their own kites can decorate them any way they like, but if the shape isn't right, they wouldn't do much flying.

A kite must be set up with the front or point facing into the wind.

The shape of a kite is what gives it the ability to fly.

After being strapped in, a hang glide kite flier is ready to go. The flight starts with a downhill run into the wind. The wind catches the kite and gives the rider the **lift** needed to fly. For the first part of the ride, the rider tries for speed and altitude. Without these, a flight may be over before it even starts. As soon as the kite gains speed and altitude, a flier can start to control the direction of flight. For a right turn, the rider leans to the right and moves the **steering bar** to the left. This tips the kite to the right and it makes a turn. To make a left turn, the rider leans left and moves the steering bar to the right.

A self-soaring pilot steers by moving the steering bar and leaning his body weight.

In kiting as in many other kinds of flying, speed and altitude work together. That is, to gain speed a flier usually has to lose altitude. To gain altitude, the kite flier has to give up some speed.

When self-soaring, a flier gains speed by tipping the front of the kite downward. As soon as enough speed has been built up, the flier leans back, raises the front of the kite, and gains altitude. The flier's skill in using wind, speed, and altitude determines how long a flight can last.

Something else every flier has to determine is when and where to make a landing. A landing should be more than just running out of altitude.

To make a good landing, a kite flier must pick a good landing spot. One with holes, bushes, rough rocks, or water is not so good. That means a rough landing. The good spot is smooth, long enough to give landing room, and slightly downhill toward the wind. To make the landing, a flier tries to lose speed and altitude slowly. A sudden loss of speed can cause a kite to **stall,** or stop. When a kite stalls, a flier may be in for a sudden landing.

A flier tries to keep the kite just above the ground until it slows to the speed at which the flier can run. At running speed the flier lets the kite down and hopes to use his legs for landing gear.

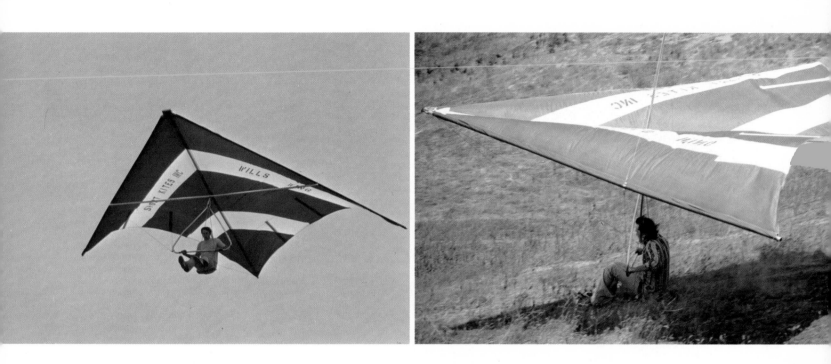

By leaning back, a kite flier can gain altitude.

Well, it's a landing, anyway.

There are some kite fliers who don't look for the right wind or hill for a chance to go soaring. This kind of flier gets altitude from the towing speed of a boat. Overwater kiting is a little like self-soaring, except the flier has to go with the tow rope. The flight follows the **wake** of the boat. The altitude can be controlled by forward-rearward tipping of the kite. And the flier must control the kite in a turn to keep from **side slipping.** Side slipping happens when a flier tips a kite into a turn too much. It can put a kite out of control and give the flier that old Greek landing. A Greek landing is hard, even on the water.

Water skis for landing gear?

Many people like to do their silent soaring in a plane. While in a **sailplane** or **glider,** fliers don't use their body weight for control. But the rules of flight for a glider are the same in many ways as those for hang gliding. To take off and get up needed speed and altitude, a **soaring** pilot may roll down a steep hill or off a cliff. Other pilots go aloft with the help of a **tow plane**. When the tow plane and glider reach a certain altitude, the pilot of the sailplane cuts loose from the tow rope. Once loose from the tow rope, the pilot circles to find rising air to keep the glider aloft. The pilot uses rising air along with changes in speed and altitude to keep the sailplane flying.

Some gliders go aloft behind a tow plane.

Gliders have long wings because that's what gives them their lift. Glider wings are shaped like other airplane wings. The wing shape gives the lift. **Flaps** on the wings and tail do the steering. The pilot controls the flaps from the **cockpit.** In the cockpit there are also instruments to show air speed, altitude, flight angle, and direction.

While a self-soaring pilot may be happy with a few hours as a flight record, some glider flights have stayed aloft as much as a day. As long as glider pilots can find rising air, they can stay aloft. Some places around the world may have rising air for hours at a time. When the glider pilot runs out of rising air, it's time to get into position for a landing.

The hang glider flier uses feet and legs as landing gear. The soaring pilot has wheels and skids. But both pilots like to land into the wind. The wind gives the glider lift while the pilot controls speed and altitude for the **landing approach.** A good landing approach at the correct speed and altitude puts a glider down *softly.* You might say that the wrong approach puts a glider down *hardly,* and that's one of those Greek landings again.

While glider pilots have instruments to show altitude, speed, and direction, the instruments are not accurate enough to depend on them for landing. During the last few feet of landing pilots must depend on their own accuracy to put the gliders back on the ground.

Since gliders have no engines, they use huge wings for their lift.

A good approach makes a good landing.

At touchdown time the landing job is almost done. At the time of touchdown the feeling of smooth flight changes into a rough and bouncing ride. Many airports used by glider pilots have rough runways. That makes the last part of the ride rough and difficult. The difficult part is keeping the glider steady and level on the runway until it slows down. If a pilot were to let one wing or the other tip too low and touch the runway, the glider could go into a spin, lose a wing, or both. Because of this the pilot must use every last bit of speed and lift to control the glider until it comes to a stop. At dead stop, the glider leans over on a wing and the flight is over.

A glider pilot tries to keep the craft level until it stops.

When there's little or no wind blowing, it's hot air balloon time. Hot air balloons are the beautiful and historical giants of the sky. History tells of two Frenchmen who flew a hot air balloon a distance of 300 feet in the year 1783. There are some who say that this was man's first flight. Others may think that the wax-feather-wing Greek men were the first fliers. But balloon people say the sport of flying and ballooning started in France around the year 1783.

Today's hot air balloon is made of a tightly woven cloth much like that used for the hang glider kite. A hang glider may be 17 to 20 feet across. An inflated balloon may be 60 to 70 feet across at the widest part.

When no wind blows, a hot air balloon goes.

When aloft, the balloon pilot and crew ride in the **gondola.** Many balloons use a gondola made of woven straw or **wicker.** The wicker is lightweight and fairly strong. Other balloonists use gondolas made of lightweight metal. The main part of the balloon, or bag, is attached to the gondola with strong cables. The gondola also holds the **propane** gas tanks and the gas burner used to heat the air in the balloon.

Balloons fly because hot air will rise above cooler air. Heating the air in the bag and making it warmer than the air around it makes the balloon rise.

Balloonists burn propane gas before and during flight to heat the air in the giant bag.

Balloon people are like most others when it comes to beauty. By using colors, decorations, and even pictures, balloonists add beauty to their sport. A professional balloon builder will let a buyer pick cloth colors and decorations, as long as the decorations don't add too much weight to the balloon.

Some balloonists build their own balloons. People who build their own balloons have to know what they're doing. Putting 1,000 square yards of cloth together into a giant bag is a giant sewing job. Besides being a giant sewing job, it has to be a good sewing job. Sewing that doesn't hold together can cut a balloon flight short—very short.

Balloonists heat the air in their balloons with propane gas burners.

A balloon getting ready to rise along with the sun.

Before flight a balloon crew is a little like a hang glider crew. There's a lot of work to do. The balloon crew lays out the bag with the hole or opening toward the wind, if there is any. A small wind helps open and inflate the bag. Any wind above 10 miles per hour is bad news—no balloon flight.

As soon as the bag is open, the crew starts a motor-driven fan. The motor-driven fan blows air into the balloon and continues the inflation. When the bag is open and partly inflated, the balloonist turns on the propane gas burner. That heats the air in the balloon and the bag starts to rise. Now the crew hangs on to keep the balloon under control until takeoff time.

During flight the balloon follows the wind and as the air in the bag cools, the balloon loses altitude. To maintain altitude the balloonist starts the propane burner and heats the air in the bag. Part of balloon competition is showing how well a pilot can reach and maintain altitude.

Balloonists learn to "steer" by watching for signs of wind at different altitudes. Clouds, smoke, and the movement of other balloons help a pilot know whether to make the balloon rise, lose altitude, or maintain level flight.

Some balloonists enter competitions, others fly just for fun. But either way, fun or competition, there's nothing else like it in the world. It's like floating on air!

An inflating balloon grows like a decorated mushroom.

Watch out, clouds, here we come.

Some people like to race with the wind while they stay on the ground. They ride the **land sailors,** the three-wheel, high-speed wind chasers. Land sailing people are called wind chasers because they chase all over the countryside trying to find a wind and a place to sail. When they find the right wind and place, they may be in a strange part of the countryside.

One strange part of the countryside to run a land sailor is the Bonneville Speedway. It's big, it's flat, and sometimes it's windy. Some sports, like the **Bonneville National Speed Trials** and ballooning shut down when the wind blows. But that's when land sailors are out setting land sail speed records.

The Bonneville Speedway in Utah is a good place for a land sailor to chase the wind.

The land sailing vehicle is a bunch of tri-angles. The frame is a triangle with wheels at each corner. The sail is a triangle with the bottom part held in place by a control rope. The driver controls the land sailor by moving the sail into, with, or out of the wind. The front wheel has a small brake and is also used for steering. But most of the steering and stopping comes from the wind on or against the sail.

To take a ride, the driver gets strapped in place. Since a land sailing machine can go very fast, even over 70 miles per hour, the seat belt is a good idea. A wrong turn can tip the vehicle. When that happens, a driver is better off in the seat than on the ground.

For competition, land sailors have different kinds of races. A few have tried to set speed records at Bonneville. Others enter a race that follows a marked course. The marked course takes the most skill, because for part of the race the driver may be trying to go sideways to the wind and even against the wind.

When the land sailor moves into or against the wind, he must **tack.** Tacking is going into the wind at zig-zag angles. By going in a zig-zag angle, a land sailor can move his vehicle into the wind, but very slowly. Tacking is a little like trying to climb a slippery hill. It's taking three steps forward and sliding back two.

Sometimes two wheels are as good as three
for the land sailors.

During competition a land sailor must be able
to move with the wind, into the wind, and
sideways to the wind.

Land sailing, like other wind sports, leads people to places like the great **Salt Desert** in Utah and the superflat **dry lakes** in Southern California. The dry lakes have plenty of wind and plenty of space. But along with plenty of wind there can be plenty of dust.

When it gets to be summer, land sailors don't use the dry lakes very much. No one uses them because it's just a little warm out there—like 110 degrees or more. When that happens, the land sailors may wish they had another big, smooth, flat place where people can race on the wind.

There's plenty of land sailing space and wind on a California dry lake. In the summer it's also h-o-t, plenty h-o-t.

It's a long way from a California dry lake and land sailing to the place where **ice boats** speed across a frozen lake. The distance between the ice lakes and the dry lakes is great, and there's a big temperature difference, too. Dry lake temperatures may be around 110 degrees. Ice lake temperatures may be zero degrees and below. But ice boaters don't mind the cold because they need a lake that's frozen solid for their sport.

An ice boat is very much like a land sailing vehicle except that it has **runners** in place of wheels. Handling the ice boat is something like land sailing, too. The driver of the ice boat wears heavy clothes and uses body weight to control the vehicle.

There's plenty of ice boat sailing space and wind on a frozen lake. It's also c-o-l-d, plenty c-o-l-d.

When the wind is right, ice boats reach some pretty great speeds over the rock-hard frozen lake. Drivers strap themselves into the boat, but they're not so tightly strapped that they can't do some leaning. A driver changes the **center of gravity** of the vehicle by leaning outside the boat. Leaning far and hard keeps the boat on the ice and lets the driver make a high-speed turn. Without leaning and changing the center of gravity, the boat would have to be slowed, or the driver might finish the turn in a slightly upside-down position. Upside down is a losing position in any race.

Ice boaters, like land sailors, may race around a closed, marked course. For part of the course the ice boater may have a wind from behind. That's when the boat picks up speed. For some of the course, the boater may have a wind from the side, and for still other parts, the driver has to tack into the wind.

Steering an ice boat around a closed course is difficult enough. What can be even more difficult is to have the wind make a sudden change of direction. If the driver isn't ready for a change in wind direction, the boat may follow the wind—off course. The driver has to find a quick way to get the boat back on course in order to finish the race.

An ice boat pilot uses body weight to control the vehicle.

During competition an ice boater must be able to move with the wind, into the wind, and sideways to the wind.

People add color, names, and decorations to their ice boats. But like so many wind-sport vehicles, ice boats have a natural beauty. The shape of the vehicle and the place where it runs all add up to something that is wonderful to see. A cloudy sky, a giant, flat, frozen lake with ice boats sending up a spray of ice make a beautiful winter picture.

So when it's cold and the ice is hard, ice boats race across the lakes. When the weather warms, and the ice is gone, the boats go into hiding until the cold weather returns. What is there to do until the cold returns?

Ice boat action: for those who like wind, speed, cold, and beauty.

Go **windsurfing**, of course. A windsurfer needs wind, but can do without ice, thank you! Windsurfers can do without the surf, too. The sport got its name because people use over-size surfboards, add sails, catch the wind, and go sailing.

The windsurf vehicle is probably harder to handle than most other types of wind vehicles. A rider controls the vehicle with body weight and sail movement. There are no wheels, skids, runners, or brakes. It's the windsurfer and the board against the wind, tide, waves, and ocean currents. It's enough to make a person feel small because a windsurfer knows there's a lot of water all around.

Like many other vehicles, a rider has to set up the vehicle before it can be used. To get ready, the windsurfer puts the mast into the surfboard, ties on ropes for control, and sets up the sail. All windsurfers are very careful about the condition of their equipment. The ocean can be a very lonely place when some equipment breaks.

To be a windsurfer a person has to be a plain **surfer**, first. Surfing teaches control of a surfboard. Then a person should also be a sailor, in order to know how to control a sail. Most important of all, a person who windsurfs has to be a swimmer. It's a long swim back to shore if a person has trouble a mile out.

Windsurfing joins two sports—sailing and surfing.

A windsurfer is careful about equipment. There's a big ocean out there.

For competition, windsurfers have races or **regattas**. There's no marked course. It's a race from here to there — and sometimes "there" is not where the wind is going. The race from here to there may be along the coast for 20 miles. A regatta can take 5 or 6 hours. Anyone who has stood up, balanced a surfboard, and controlled a flapping sail for 6 hours knows how tiring it can be. But with a good wind, the regatta may not take so long. With little or poor wind, the regatta may end at some spot along the coast where a windsurfer has to drop out. One rule windsurfers have is, "Finish the regatta before dark." After dark, it might be a little hard to find a lost windsurfer.

For a person who wants to do it all, a windsurfer can join other surfers. There's really nothing to it. All the rider has to do is get out beyond the surf. That's problem number one. The next step is turning back into the surf. That's problem number two, especially if the wind is blowing in the wrong direction. Then there is the wait for the right **set of waves**. That's problem number three—how to hold the windsurfer still and wait. Problem four is catching the right wave in a set. Problem five is riding the wave. Six, watch out for the other surfers. And lucky seven, if it is lucky, make it to shore. There's really nothing to it!

What a way to go to sea! A surf sailing regatta.

What a way to come back from the sea! A surf sailor sailing on the surf.

Each wind sport has its own challenge. The hang glide kite flier sails into space from the top of a hill or cliff. A glider pilot uses wings to find rising air that can give the vehicle speed and altitude. A water ski kite flier sails through the air while looking down on the wake of a high-speed boat. Land sailors speed through the great deserts as they chase the hot, dry winds. Balloonists fly silently across the sky and ice boaters flash over frozen lakes. And the windsurfer silently goes out to sea, holding the surfboard and sail into the wind. For all, it's the challenge of silent speed or silent flight. It's racing on the wind.

It's racing on the wind.

Glossary/Index

(Page number indicates where
the word first appears in the book.)

47

Ruth and Ed Radlauer, authors of over seventy books for young people are graduates of UCLA. They have worked as teachers, school administrators, reading specialists, and instructors in creative writing. Their books have been in the areas of science, language, social studies, and, more recently, high-interest reading materials. Books in the Sports Action series include *On the Drag Strip, Scramble Cycle, Buggy-Go-Round, On the Sand, Chopper Cycle, Horsing Around, On the Water, Salt Cycle, Bonneville Cars, Motorcycle Mutt, Foolish Filly,* and *Racing on the Wind.*

Along with their three children, two horses, a motorcycle, a dog, and an ancient cat, the Radlauers live in La Habra, California.

Picture credits: Photographs on pages 33, 35, and 37 supplied by Susan Sprague of the INDRA, Northeast, Pennsylvania.

Library of Congress Cataloging in Publication Data

Radlauer, Edward
    Racing on the wind.
    SUMMARY: Advice for participants in wind sports involving hang glide kites, sailplanes, gliders, hot air balloons, land sailors, ice boats, and wind surf vehicles.
    1. Aeronautical sports—Juvenile literature. 2. Sailing—Juvenile literature. I. Radlauer, Ruth Shaw, joint author. II. Title. Title.
GV757.R32   796   73-17055
ISBN 0-531-02681-7